Women's
Rites,
Rights,
Writes

Women's Rites, Rights, Writes

Bonnie Bostrom, Carla Christianson,
Michele Cuomo, Barbara Martin,
Barbara Poirer, Juanita Remien, Kim Roley,
Mia Self, Paula Pam Wainwright

Contents

Introduction

When Michele Marie invited me to create a poetry workshop with her, I responded with alacrity. Then I panicked. I had done many workshops in the past, but never on zoom. We had worked together on some projects that were poetry - based book creation. This would be something very different, but I was excited to work with her again, and looked forward to the adventure.

Because Michele's vision was to build a safe environment for women to express their thought in poetry, and to allow the experience to unfold organically, it allowed for a wonderful freedom. We planned to assess the talent in the group and keep participants at a minimum. There were ten of us. We began by offering the workshop every Saturday for a month. We really did not know what to expect. We certainly did not expect to be bowled over by the work the women produced. But we were. When the first month was complete, there was a strong impetus on everyone's part to continue. So we worked for another full month, once a week. During that time, we suggested that we should write with the goal of creating a book. The women went to work!!!

This book is the result of women being open, sharing their work, receiving feedback from each other, and risking to go ever deeper into their lives, retrieving images, and finding the right words. The workshop morphed into a place of self-discovery, transformation, and self-appreciation.

We had two guests; Elizabeth Burns gave us a day in which we benefitted from her expertise as a professor of poetry and literature, and as a widely published author. You can read her comments included in the Pre-Publication Praise section.

Henry Long, poet/painter/photographer, is our editor. He presented valuable insights about self-editing and let the writers know what to expect from his editing. He was able to provide gentle guidance on their finished pieces. You can read his reflections on the Editor's page.

The writers? I invite you to open this book, open your heart, and let their voices bring themselves to you.

—Bonnie Bostrom

Editor's page

To the poets of Women's Rights Rites Writes, thank you all for the opportunity to read, hear, and live with your poetry, and for the trust in my editorial suggestions. Being with your words and having such intimacy with them has been an honor as well as an inspiration.

What follows is "Editing Women," a poem born from the process of being allowed to peer into your thoughts, your lives, and your unique reflections. I encourage you all to keep writing, keep patient observation, keep asking questions, keep listening to your inner voices, and remain in awe of everything!

> Love and Gratitude,
> —Henry

Henry Long, editor

Henry Long was born and raised in the small, anthracite coal mining town of Ashley, Pennsylvania. He is an artist and photographer, and has self-published 14 poetry chapbooks. He has given hundreds of poetry readings over the past 45 years. His poems and short stories have appeared irregularly in print and online journals, and he has received recognition for his art, photography, and poetry, including the 2002 Individual Artistic Fellowship Grant from the Delaware Division of the Arts as an Emerging Professional in Poetry.

"Uncommon Constants," a collaborative effort with the poet and artist Bonnie Bostrom, was published in 2022 by The Canelo Project. In 2024, he was one of three guest editors for issue #99 of the arts and literary journal Cholla Needles, "The Witnesses Project," where his poetry and photography also appeared.

Henry and his two daughters live among the beautiful trees and low-rolling hills of Pike Creek, Delaware. They are happy.

Editing women

First, I was asked, and accepted the kind invitation to poetic intercourse and communion. My editorial task, if interpretation of dreams and endeavoring to read between the lines and peer behind the masks can be called such an undertaking, came with gentle and perfect timing.

> The setting: Alone at my kitchen table, cat nearby, windows open to the wind, children away to the beach for the week.

> I worked the mornings and graveyard shifts, reciting the women's passages in between cups of black coffee and kerosene.

Poetry is a time machine,

looking back in water each night

at the flow of the river that rushes us here,

accepting the gray silk gift from the visitor,

sliding gracefully beneath cool cotton sheets

of the tomb— the remedy for our silenced pain

is so much like a womb, with the shedding

and gestation and the shotgun wedding

of our grand, climacteric bloom.

Words say so much more

than words alone can say.

I've heard it said of men

that women are such a mystery to them.

Maybe they're reading the wrong poems.

Love and Gratitude,

—Henry

Juanita Remien

Juanita wants to preserve the earth and its inhabitants, and sees spirit in, and interconnection between, all things and beings. She describes how humans, plants, and animals get along. Her work appears in The Witnesses Project. In addition to poems, she has published scientific and environmental articles.

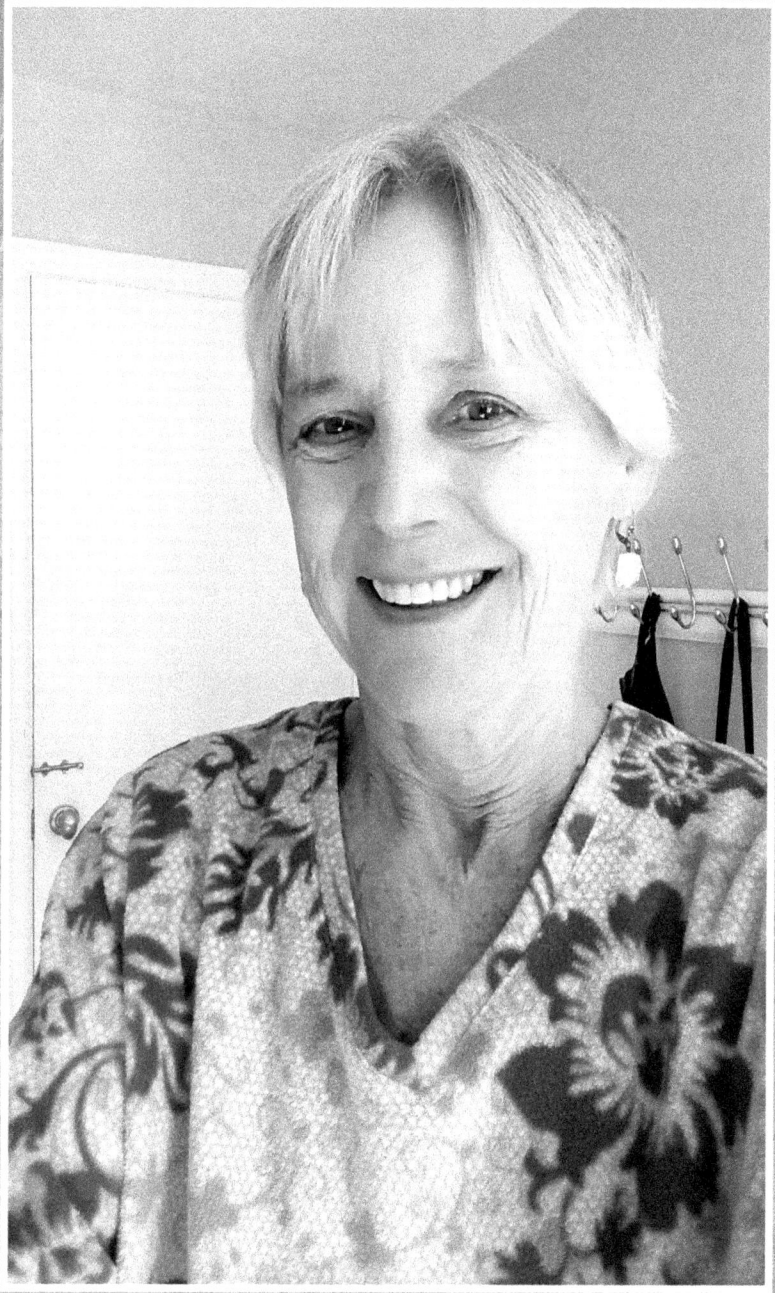

Finding Freedom

In the water I am free
A member of the dolphin club
Buoyant, unencumbered
Longitudinal stretch of trunk
  and limbs
Effortless gliding through liquid.

Head turns rhythmically side to side
Breathing in a gulp of air by mouth
Blowing bubbles out into the water
My body lets go.

Pushing off the end of the pool
I am no longer in a race
  with the swimmer in the next lane.
There is no time. There is no winner.

Swimmers are evolving
Hand paddles and foot flippers
  augment already capable limbs.
Earbuds lend an illusory solitude
The serious swimmer demands upgrades.

But my body is enough
Just as it is, without trappings
Audible cracks in joints, restrictions and pains
Dissolve in the water

Mental turmoil transcended, I am saved!
Baptized by total immersion
 again and again.
I keep swimming.

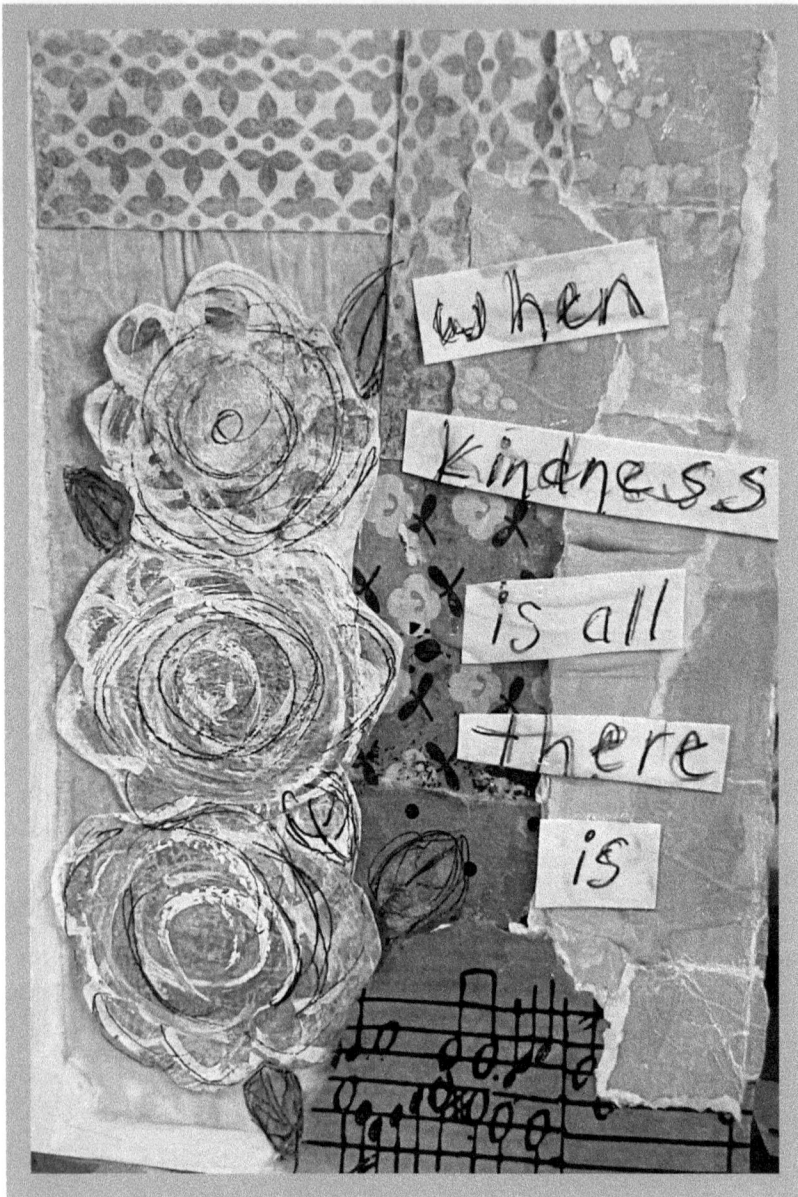

when
kindness
is all
there
is

Sliding Gracefully into Phase 3

wistful wisteria winks at me
flowering quince quiets the wind
forsythia forsakes all others for me
mama mahonia dries my tears

rose creek abelia hosts a swarm of bees
headed blithely to the butterfly bush

agile azalea asks nothing of me
rambunctious red rhododendron waves
magnolia magnetizes my nose
flowering cherry chants in the early morning

sultry sasanqua shifts in the soil
shows off her white winter flowers

a snake creeps down and I step forward
to seven stars
stepping back I ride the tiger
then turn to sweep the lotus
bending the bow, I shoot the tiger.

La naturaleza cruel

Un lince rojo
viene a mi casa
voy a domarle

Gato afuera
persigue al pájaro
tratando de volar

Una vez que voló
ahora plumas arrancadas
poder lo dejó

Gato salvaje
rey de la selva de jardin
le gusta cazar

Luchar es inútil
el pobre pájarito
jugado a la muerte

Cruel Nature

A bobcat
arrives at my house
I am going to tame him.

Cat outside
pursues the bird
trying to fly.

Once he flew
now feathers plucked out
he has no power.

Savage cat
King of the garden jungle
Likes to hunt.

Fighting is futile
the poor bird
played to the death.

Los cuervos rebeldes

(escrito durante las protestas en Portland, 2020)

Encima en el cielo, lleno de nubes negras
En las ramas del abedul llorón
Un asesinato de cuervos se reúnen
Oyen tambores y gritos en atmósfera tensa.
Tratan de mantener la calma

Los cuervos rebeldes vuelan en oleadas
 en formas determinadas
Se acercan al centro, juntarse con su tribu
Graznidos se mezclan con gritos de multitud
Plumas negras apoyan a piel negra.

The Rebellious Crows

(written during the Portland protests, 2020)

Above in the sky, full of black clouds

In the weeping birch tree branches

A murder of crows gathers

Hearing drums and shouts

  in a tense atmosphere

They try to stay calm

The rebellious crows fly in waves

  in determined formation

Approaching downtown, reuniting with

  their tribe

The crows' caws blend with the cries

  of the crowd

Black feathers support black skin.

Pine Siskin, Bird Teacher

Sky lightened moments ago
Weary, blurry eyes open
Zombie march to coffee pot.

Outside I sit, waiting
In the mid-summer dream
Song sparrow arrives on time
He knows the drill
Usual morning trill
  from his perch on the jasmine trellis.

Soaking up smooth, cool air sounds
Crows, wiser than they sound
Neighbor's hacking cough resounds,
  comes in rounds
Between song sparrow and train horn.

Traffic hum on Highway 26 insists
  on getting louder
Rhythm is broken by a shrill siren
All is not well.

The pine siskin cruises by my eye
Touches down on cool patio tile nearby
Showing off his chevron-patterned brown body
Carrying streaks of subtle amber
  on wings and tail.

Eternity passes, he still rests
No movement in his breast
Right foot juts out from under him
  at an odd angle
Head down, frozen in place

Are these his final moments?
I sit vigil
Closing my eyes, we silently bond

I drift off, time goes by
Opening my eyes just in time
To see my new friend fly.

Paula Pam Wainwright

Paula retired in 2019 after a long career as an RN (over 43 years), spent in both end-of-life and Hospice care, as well as in Behavioral health prior to retirement. She has lived in two of the most beautiful parts of this country: Sonoma County, CA, and the Mountains of Western NC, and currently resides in Asheville, NC, all of which are most dear to her heart.

In addition to a long career in Nursing, Paula was trained as a psychotherapist in California, and although licensed, never got to practice due to a sudden move to FL in 2006 for a variety of family-related reasons.

In retirement, Paula spends most of her time making Art, doing some writing, and making time with her granddaughter Caliana, who is her "miracle "baby, having been born at a wee 1lb 4oz. (Today, Caliana is entering 2nd grade and is thriving.) Paula is also blessed with another granddaughter, Anaka, who will be turning three on this winter Solstice.

In addition to the above, Paula has found true spiritual community in the Meher Baba family here in Asheville and has a rich and profound community of friends for which she is eternally grateful.

The natural beauty of the mountains in Western NC is incredibly nourishing, and Paula can also be found frequenting the area's variety of lakes, rivers, and pools with her "mermaid friends."

Each Night

Each night, I sit and pedal on that bicycle without handlebars, against that bench for support. I pedal for close to an hour, to keep alive, momentum, some movement as this is a saving grace for me, moving on, forward, moving Somewhere!

As I pedal, I watch YouTube art videos, trying to permeate my being with color and beauty, for I believe they will be an infusion of color and charm, especially when such chaos explodes in my life daily. I have always struggled with keeping up; things always appear to be moving faster than I, for as long as I can remember!

I find myself wanting to compare notes with others, ask them, "Have you been challenged like I have been?" I find such solace when meeting others who can relate to my struggle.

I once wanted to write a book, "The Pain of the Unmattered People." Why do I remember that now? Perhaps it belongs on my bucket list!

I look around at my surroundings and try to find a space or two to make sweet, calm, beautiful. Just that thought alone calms me. I need to have little corners like these, in my life, in my heart, a place to find composure and repose. Those spaces that remind me that "all is well as it should be and can be wherever I am!"

This Day

This day, a sadness arises like a whisper. I wanted to be there for you, but you are not letting me in. In your own way, you told me you were done for the day. I know it is not personal; it's just your way of asserting yourself until the very end. It feels so abrupt, like a slap! I wanted softer and gentler than this.

At the end of her life, my Mom gave me that gift, surrendered her care into my hands, as an honor, and I was able to help her gently until the very end, through her last breath in this world. This will not be how it will happen for us.

Trust was always an issue that rose between us like a silent flame.

I can travel back in time and see it so clearly now. I want the deepest connection, and you want to protect your heart. I wanted to be able to walk you home.

Carla Christianson

Carla is passionate about defending the environment, democracy, and equity for all people. She is a retired entrepreneur, a lover of poetry, a vegetarian, and a lifelong learner. Carla and her husband live in Ormond Beach, Florida. She was encouraged by Bonnie Bostrom to write poetry and has found delight in the practice.

Looking Back

She looked back.
The path disappeared,
at the top of the hill, around a corner, over the horizon.
She had memories, mostly vague, no longer in any order.
Her little feet swaddled in Bunny Bread wrappers,
entombed in rubber boots, made a path in snow.
Still falling flakes or swirling drifts quickly obscured those steps.
Her feet followed the water's edge on many beaches.
Footprints in sand washed away by tides, hungry waves,
and rewritten by shore birds.

On boats trailing waves tracked her path,
til the searching circles lost their urge to seek and simply died,
lapping powerless against the land.

The forest called her, and she walked among trees,
the maple, birch, and pine of the north woods.
Under the Southern Cross, she visited
eucalyptus, acacia, melaleuca, and gum trees.
She found a home among live oaks, sabal palm, and magnolias.
Each tree an inspiration. No tree ever noticed her presence.
No mark to record her passing.
Yet she saw how the journey had made a mark on her.

The path, not what was pictured,
not what was planned, but more than the child
could have dreamed of as she caught snowflakes on her tongue,

gathered seashells on the beach, paddled a canoe,
or trimmed a sail.

Looking back, she is filled with awe.
It was not her voyage but fellow travelers, the teachers,
the lovers, the children, the elders,
the listeners, the singers, the speakers, the poets.
Now she is an elder and realizes all were teachers.
She, never not the student.

Each Night

Each night I make a meal to share

then eat before those who seek to explain

the world as it unfolded today.

Each night, I hear them opine as I try to escape their words.

Each night, my screens are there,

like worry beads to help me find a state of grace.

Each night, I keep up, then recoil and play those games.

I scream in silence, I weep, I lose or win.

Each night, helplessness, anger, and outrage eat away my heart

while we eat a bowl of popcorn, a frozen treat

with every cell of me on high alert.

Each night, head bowed, eyes averted, I see

what I never wanted to see while trying to perfect

   a dissociative fugue state.

Black Snake

Draped casually in tall grass,
I thought it was a whip; intricately woven black leather.
Following the flowing length, yellow eyes met mine.
Mouth open, head swaying, his slow twisting became
my skin writhing, a twisting grip in my belly,
as fear settled like dense fog.
I backed slowly away.
This is my space
invaded.

Deep beyond thought lies this hatred.
The path from door to world is terror-filled.
Weeks pass and fear slipped away
pulling guarded tension with it.

Back at the edge of woods, my steps
startle a shadowy, slender brush stroke.
Dark ink flows through crisp oak leaves
with the ease of milk sliding among flakes in a bowl.
Slithering under withered palm fronds, camouflage complete.
My power, my victory so fleeting.
Freedom vanished.
The apparition owned my home.

Flow of the River

Rivers are layered, textured, complicated.
Wind, rain, clouds, sun
paint self-portraits on the surface.
But beneath,
the inner life of a river is an
unknowable current;
a force that can be rich with life
or obscure painful debris.

A river moves like
a limber, stretching cat,
a paw reaching far
beyond her grasp,
rubbing her belly over soft, rippled sand
or deftly sliding over jolting rocks and logs,
crouched low,
prowling toward a far-off sea.

A river can be filled to overflowing,
lunging without restraint,
racing forward, outward,
oozing into forbidden spaces,
seeking limits and eventual retreat.
Beware of the danger of too much.

A river in times of dryness,
to shield against the sun,
curls in upon itself.
Eddies or pools,
movement slows,
almost stilled,
character changes,
muddied, maybe hidden.
Beware the danger of not enough.

Life, like a river,
can change in a flash or
so slowly, alteration is unnoticed—
but always,
always, it is moving,
moving,
always moving,
and that far-off sea
comes closer every day.

At the River

The river is mesmerizing.
In the afternoon,
before the sun
snuggles with the trees
leaking long, low rays between
fronds and foliage,
before the sky becomes ablaze
with sherbet streaks
of mango, pineapple, and raspberry,
she slips golden coins
from a luminescent basket
made from firefly wings
onto the ruffled watery surface.

Those glittering discs are
a gleeful giggle to watch.
Dolphins skip golden stones with joy.
The tiny jumping fish scatter them and
ancient pelicans glide above the dancing light
then crash the surface pretending to fill
their saggy pouches with liquid sequins.
A sudden breeze may shatter
the shining bits into minute glints
as shore birds and turtles stand watch.

Inevitably, shadows creep down to water's edge
to tidy up the faded light,
tuck away the last tint of color,
and smudge the lines between land and stream
quelling the dazzle.

When the river is silent and dark,
fairy lights decorate the sky.
Sister Luna arises from her ocean slumber,
her hand filled with silver coins
to slip onto the liquid black velvet.
Happily they play among the ripples
as she climbs a charcoal sky.
Tiny mirrors record her journey.

Water has fierce power
to nourish or destroy.
Alone with my grief,
in this darkness, my heart can only pray
these sacred coins,
gold and silver,
offerings to the river gods,
will grant us peace.

Kim Roley

Kim has been writing poetry since she was quite young and has found it to be a lifelong friend. She shares her work online and in poetry groups and hopes to publish a chapbook soon. She lives happily with her family in Virginia and attempts to write every day.

Each Night

Each night
we take required meds
brush our teeth
bow heads to pray.

Each night
we are
(or should be)
grateful for another day

Each night
we sleep
dreamless or dreamer the same
each night in hope
of another day.

Green

Jealousy was never green.

Jealousy was blue— deep ocean blue eyes
And summer blonde hair.

All curves, like the dunes on the beach
Where I sat and watched you

Run into a future
That didn't include me.

Lost Poem

There truly was a poem.
But it's gone now,
disappeared into the
unending blue screen
of a power outage.
Written in the box, no backup
of scratch paper, no ink was used
to birth these words.
And they're still gone.
Someday, they may come up
through the whiteness—
black letters bleeding onto the white screen,
night appearing as the ghost
in your machine.

Please, take them.
They are my gift to you.

Reaching Out Blindly,
I Send You Water

I think I wrote you this poem,
but
I don't know who you are
or where.

The leaves curl upward when they sense rain coming.
Cup your hands to capture the manna that falls— someone,
somewhere, hungers. Someone thirsts.

The water gurgles to itself as it travels down the gutter
to the sea— there's a story underneath, but it runs too quickly by
for you to capture more than a trickle of words as you reach.

One night, she bathed in blue water with bubbles.
She said she was taking a bath in the sky.
Remembering the womb, she smiles upwards.

I want to wear my longest swirly skirt and walk along the edge
of the sea barefoot and lean forward into the ocean, drinking it in.
I am craving salt; I want the brine to dry in ridges on my skin.

I'm sending you this poem—
like a paper boat upon the sea sent by a child
who has never understood a storm or seen a wreck,
in hopes that you will understand the why,
and send it back.

Rapunzel, Thinking

Why must I come down,
she thinks.
Why must I let down my hair?
Why can't I be allowed
my time
   my space
      my books and birds?

Why am I not allowed
to be satisfied
with small things
  and silence
  and viewing the arc of Heaven
through a tower window?

Why are these things
I have learned
and loved
now deemed insufficient?

Why, oh WHY,
must he pull my hair?

Bonnie Bostrom

Bonnie has written fourteen books, either solo or in collaboration with other poets and artists. She is currently working on two other projects. Her writing has appeared online and in print, and can be found on Amazon, through her website, bonniebostrom.com, and on Facebook at Bostrom Arts.

Final Things

The mandrake root gave birth,

new stars were thrown

with Heidegger's ghost,

into a sea of sky.

Every ocean sent a wave;

dolphins, flying into turgid air

like great dark birds

looking for shore.

I flew in their wake,

followed them to a dim,

and distant star.

Life was folding its hand.

Stars die, leave their light,

a luminous, pitiless path;

I am weary, tired of the fire.

My feet burn.

Sister Death

My death draws near,
Her gentle fingers poke,
evoke, release
pieces of pain, once hidden.

Forbidden globe-glass tears
roll down my cheeks
leave streaks of wet;
translucent hail.

Melted, she sips them, smiles,
takes old hurts into her shade,
forges, fashions,
makes them into forgetting.

She is surrender-soft, hums
a familiar tune I almost remember;
I am a small child in new darkness,
trying so hard to hear.

I hold hot breath, hold back hail,
listen beyond a sounding heart
for my father's absent voice
calling my name.

Broncs and Bones

Secrets stored marrow deep
Creep into my dreams
Surface in unbidden
Carefully hidden memories.

Visions on half-life thorazine shuffle
Sideways, insinuate into consciousness,
Then retreat when I turn
My real body over in bed.

Fact: The universe makes two complete turns every trillion years.
Fiction: It takes a trillion years to shake brilliant tracers,
Imprints the dreams leave;
Impressionistic neon brain-painting.

I sort a collection of mental photos
Conjure compositions to feel drunk
With pain, dangerous and dark,
Red-hot with life.

I am a penitente.
Flagellations, transparent wounds,
Leave no marks;
Pain is always invisible.

Pictures incised, indelibly
Scribed on my heart's retina send
Blood memory into a map of flesh;
I'm an autonomous ambulatory being

Asleep in delicious solitude,
(A practice place for dying),
I see an infinite exfoliation of time;
Live theatre in the round.

It takes a trillion years to make two turns.
I ride this planet like a rodeo cowgirl
Or like my dad on Muddy Waters,
Borger, Texas, 1946.

His free arm raised handsome high
In forever salute to his future,
There, frozen in mid air, horse and rider
Will never come to ground.

The Visitor

We had a late, surprise snow
So the streets were wet
The air bitter.
It was early morning after
Dark had disappeared into day
When the doorbell rang.

There she was, outside my metal,
Locked, screen door
Probably sixty, wrapped
Caesar style in
An ancient gray blanket,
Shivering,
Begging for matches.

Fear did not unlock the screen.
Wait here, I said.
I brought matches,
One oatmeal cookie, bottled water.
She seemed grateful,
Standing there in yellow
Rubbered hospital socks.

Even though she turned,

Disappearing into her life,

She is still at my door.

After Dylan

(Written upon reading his poem "Love in the Asylum")

In one blaze-brilliant line

he set fire to all the stars;

dark had no hold on him.

Galaxies gave bright new life

to a thousand constellations.

He used them to burn words of fire

seared them directly on my brain.

I consume his poem;

it flames, breaks beauty

into being as my eyes

acclimate to naked light.

Barbara Poirier

Mashantucket Pequot elder and matriarch, fledgling artist, writer, and poet, Barbara Poirier has enjoyed weaving baskets, crocheting, and macrame'. Most recently, she has been inspired by and encouraged to paint by dear artist friends Lucinda Lickver and Bonnie Bostrom. She lives in Stuart, FL, and Niantic, CT, with her husband, Ray, and their Cavapoo, Gigi Luna.

Ghost

Softly, the night descended on us.

You asked if you could hold my hand.

I, amazed and delighted at the simple question, took your hand, strong and smooth in mine.

We walked toward the sound of the waves, crashing upon the sand.

It was dark.

We had trouble finding our way at first,

iron fences and padlocked gates kept us from our destination.

Suddenly, you stop walking and turn to utter words of awe and thanks for the moment in time.

Warm ocean breezes kissed our faces as we gazed upon the moon and stars scattered along the night sky.

We talked.

Questions.

Answers, sometimes hesitant.

I search your moon-lit face; gaze into your eyes.

What do you want from me?

What shall I give you?

As softly as it began, the night ended.

An embrace, a chaste kiss,

a promise of more tender moments like this.

I never saw you again.

Pillows and Stones

Stay soft around the struggles of this wondrous,
at times hard and heavy life

Like Sisyphus you carry the weight

uphill, both ways

Be soft within your heart

Do not construct a wall of stone

as if that will smother the pain

Only a pillow will do

Rest your head there

Lay down your burdens

Breathe into presence.

Walk to the water's edge

where the pebbles are tumbled wet with seawater

These stones held in soft palms run through your fingers
like tiny gemstones

And disappear into the waves that wash onto the sand.

Go to the forest, quiet but for the sounds of nature

Turn over the flat stone to see what is beneath

and know that the stone becomes soil

and the pillow becomes but fluff that is strewn about
like the seeds of the dandelion.

Impermanence is soft and hard like pillows and stones.

Looking Back in Water

Riding rogue waves is hard.

They are nightmarish and unpredictable.

Their billowing forms swell to great heights, recede,

and then suddenly take off in a new direction,

breaking away from the ordinary currents, winds, and tides.

They roll under me.

I am surfing, floating, and finally, floundering

in the quivering, glimmering sea foam.

I am breathless.

I am lost in the sea of dreams,

asleep under the water.

Genocide in Gaza

Listen!

What do you hear?

The sounds of a mother

as she buries her starved, dead child

Howling!

Everything Green

My maternal ancestors were born in the eastern woodlands.

I was, too.

Maple, elm, and oak are abundant here, though their green
leaves dry up and drop to the ground in the fall.

A great wind will render these trees naked in the blink of an eye.

Black Ash once thrived here.

My grandmother knew exactly where to find it, along with
other precious green plants and medicinal herbs.

She would wait until winter, when the trunk was still heavy
with sap.

Chopping down the tree, she would drag it to a stream in the
swamp where it would soak over the winter.

In the spring, she would pound the bark to make splints
for her baskets,

carrying on the traditions of her mother and grandmothers.

Black Ash is no longer found here.

The emerald ash borer feeds on the pointy green leaves
and has caused a relentless blight.

Emerald is also a shade of green.

In the west are the enormous redwood and mesmerizing windswept cedar.

Lush green palms are native to the south, and the lovely banyans sometimes form a canopy across the roadway— a bower of cool shade as respite from the hot southern sun.

Pine, fir, and spruce are evergreen in the north.

At the heart of this country is the mesquite and willow.

Cacti are not trees, but the saguaro can grow as big in the desert.

They are all green sentinels marking time.

Evergreen is nourishing spinach, kale, and broccoli.

Christmas trees severed from the ground, dragged home, and decorated with ornaments and baby's breath.

Green is the Grinch, Green Goblin, and Hulk.

Fantasy stays green for me.

Money backs are green here.

So is envy.

Pond scum lies like a blanket on the still water.

Lillies rest delicately on their green pads.

Moss was growing in my house gutters until the men came with their tall ladders, plucked it out, and washed it away.

Barbara Martin

Charming daughter, sister, mother, grandmother, significant lover, bingo player, and retired teacher. When not spinning words into poetry, Barb spends her time living, laughing, loving and learning in the Colorado mountains.

The Tomb

As I stepped inside the gates of St. Louis Number 1, rain fell gently on the path. Wide-eyed and wonderstruck, I gazed at the multitude of angels, cherubic, divine, wonton, forlornly guarding the countless souls of centuries-old residents of time and the French Quarter.

Appearing at the tomb of Marie Laveau, voodoo queen, keeper of plentiful powers of mesmerism and manipulation, I was struck with astonishing emotions of reverent awe.

Concoctor of Creole potions, a sister in the freedom of slaves, ritualistic healer, and alleged assister to the sick and dying, advisor, and spiritual guide.

Gasping at the infinite X's carved on the tomb by devout followers, in hopes of wishes granted, I whispered to her. Queen, sorceress, freedom fighter, magical, mystical voodoo legend......

Our secrets remain safe with you.

Gone

Like black roses, my love has become brittle cold dry

Frustrated to speak dark secrets from my once warm inviting lips

Faces like lies turn away as bitter reality reveals the ugly truth

Unable to say goodbye or know how you feel

Perhaps I never will.

Tupperware

Dishwashing is ugly, for fuck's sake!

Okay... Forks, spoons, knives jumbling, refusing any easy sort.

Then the Tuppers come in with abounding abundance!
What the hell?

Where are all the lids that match all this madness?

Now twitching, stirring warm, mellow tea with the rogue
spoon that refused to go into that hot mess...

Shall I keep it on the honey-soaked napkin or toss it into the
dish abyss?

This dilemma can wait until tomorrow.

Working Mothers

Noise

Dirty diapers

Fighting and cleaning

Too many TV dinners

Wash rinse spin

Wash rinse spin

Dry

Yanks

It totally yanks my chain and gets my haunch hair bristly
quick when some guy talks over me to cut me off!

Not certain if it's my delivery, my woman warrior strength,
this frickin speech impediment, or the content of my
passionate words......

Just know that you can't shut me up, shut me down, or shut
me off!!!! I have something to say!

Michele Cuomo

Michele, like Langston Hughes, is tired of waiting for the world to become good, beautiful, and kind, but finds solace in the company of poets. She lives with her husband, Paul, in Winter Springs, Florida.

Milk and Kale

The lake is milk
at dusk

Below the surface
Seminole and Cracker blood
mingled

Suffering smoothed by waves
and rocks

We are reminded by
a fading sign
at the shore

We did not know them:
it does not hurt

The sea is kale
a woman brings her children
to eat the green foam

and is turned away

The woman is salt
she took a look back

Gray Silk

(After "White Apples" by Donald Hall)

When my mother had been dead a while

I woke with her voice in my ear

Sheets shucked from the bed

A rustling just past the door

Gray silk and anisette

And if she had whispered for me to come

I would have worn the dress she loved

And brushed my hair

Each Night

Each night we sit as the sun has its last rage and then surrenders back down.

Each night the cat cries more more and I cry you ate you ate.

Each night we leave the dishes wet on the rack and catch the crumbs. I close the light, you turn it back on.

Each night we stare at separate screens, but you call me over to share, and I kiss the top of your head.

Each night we sleep touching fingertips.

Each night, no, it was only one night last week. I dreamt I was with my mother, and when I woke up, I did not know of this time anymore. I was back with her, and I woke up naked.

Where am I? Who are you?

Each night I try the New York Times method to get to sleep. Think random thoughts: elephant, bird, accounting, wherewithal, singers, dogs, facelifts, hunters. It's supposed to mimic what happens in our brain when we start to fall asleep. I make it complicated, somehow.

Each night I put one hand on my heart and the other on my belly and say to myself— it's alright it's alright.

Each night we have to fix the bed. The sheets come undone. I forget, and have to be roused one more time.

Each night I look in the mirror and smile to avoid seeing my face sunken.

Each night I take a moment to look for the moon above the palm trees. Sometimes there is a star.

Each night I collect the plumeria flowers from the sidewalk and place them in the shot glass on the table. They wilt the next day, but oh, the scent.

A Morning Walk in my Own Head

(after Adelaide Crapsey)

Listen:

A dove's soft coo,

A mockingbird's retort.

With each step, bones crunch and bark breaks—

Silence.

Her Seasons

Born in the rain:

blood and placenta seeping,

springing flowers.

She takes first steps, she speaks cat's tongue.

A wild tree, she grows unevenly,

ungainly, many falls.

After many summers,

she is a fern in reverse,

curling back down to the wet earth.

Her winter is long, but mild.

The gray skies good.

Lightning strikes white.

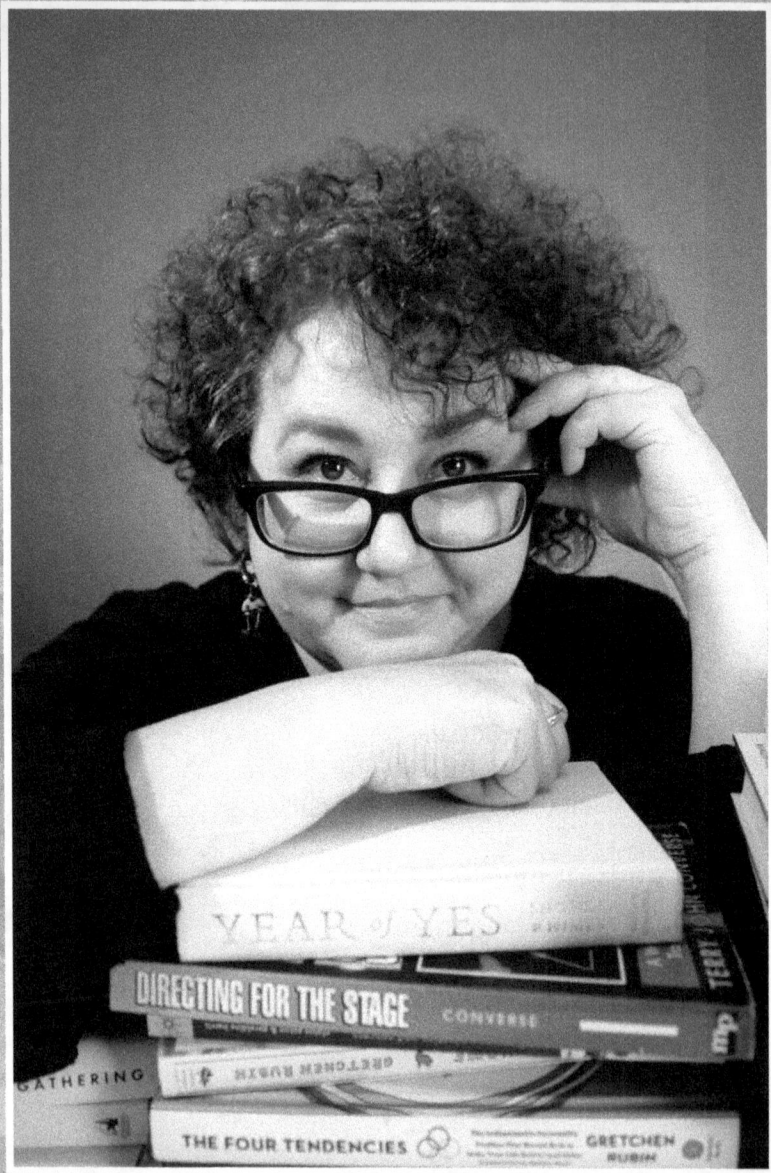

Mia Self

Mia is a theatre director, teacher, and occasional writer living in Raleigh, NC. Her performance career began with Poetry Alive!, a national touring company out of Asheville, NC., in the early 90s and her love affair with language has continued to this day.

Enmeshment

Compensatory strategies and

Maladaptive behaviors and

Plain old bad habits

Float through me

Like dandelion fluff,

Like feathers,

Like dryer lint.

Once plucked, the concepts

Pinned to an internal corkboard then

Tied with button thread,

With sock weight wool,

With sinews pulled from flesh

To behaviors and

To habits and

To hopes

That make me wonder

If the label is bound to some crime committed.

Have the threads and

Pins and

Phrases

Wound themselves together

Into a web,

A crocheted nest,

A knitted mesh

Of judgments

To hold me together

Or to hold me in?

Judith Butler. Again.

I'm obsessed with Judith Butler again after all these
years. I read Thinking Through the Body and wrestled
with and felt the truth of her academic reality, surrounded
by men aping womanly sensibilities to maintain the status
quo, to maintain their power in a changing world. And my
presentation partner pissed beyond reason that it "wasn't
a feminist book at all" because "where in the hell was the
bra burning?" And my paltry defense that feminism wasn't
about the bra, it was about power and place and respect
and personhood and all that could be argued and
defended, whether or not Judith Butler was wearing a bra.

Now Judith Butler has surrendered to a broader scope.
Their embrace of non-binary pronouns, their awe at
enacted "girl" and "boy," and their inability to make
sense of either in an embodied way is both hilarious and
deeply touching.

I understood "girl," for I had borrowed my mother's
Candies and pranced on the front porch aping Sandy's
black spandex and leather-clad Pink Lady transformation.
I practiced the full-leg smushing of stolen cigarette butts
with as much precision as an eight-year-old can muster.
I understood "girl," but I couldn't "do" girl. I wasn't built
for it nor inclined to fluff for it. I was "girl," but always
with failing marks.

I understood "boy" with the in-built desires to throw a ball, drive the lawn mower in tightly orchestrated patterns, or to cook, but only with live flames. I understood "boy," and could do "boy" better than "girl," though my heart wasn't in it. It pained me for I knew that secretly, and not so secretly, my father had wished I were a boy. Or, at least, that's what the whispers of the women in my family shared with me. Shared with compassion, with longing, with sadness. So I aped the men around me and tried to catch the ball and lift the heavy thing. I was a disappointment, even to myself.

The trouble with gender, Judith Butler might add, is that it's possible to know the expectations, to understand the defining parameters, and yet be equally aware that success is impossible because you weren't designed for this game.

A Texas City

It was a chapel
Remember?
We prayed before the Rothkos

From this distance and time
It seems scented with warmed skin
And possibilities

But it was only
The epic scale of paint on canvas
Caressed by the light of the clerestory

The overwhelming silence
Drenched that sacred space
Around and between us

We wished our flesh
Might dwell entwined like
Brushstrokes across taut fabric

In the end
We surrendered
To the void of silence

Gift

Stop bracing for your failures
Don't offer grudging trust
Hold still and wait
Breathe

Allow yourself the space
To be
To try
To fail

To remain in the staggering
And the struggle
To make ugly, halting steps

Then to praise
The janky, awkward mess
You have become

Find the joy
As you pursue
The next
The better

Celebrate
Yourself
As you become

The Remedy

The lid removed from the murky cauldron

A pool, dark gray, warming within

A paddle captures a clot of blackened green

A hand pulls taut

A smear of heat in short, sharp strokes

The bright, breathtaking tear of release

The press of skin into skin

The tenderness of missing fur

A shock of alcohol

A diminishing sting

A slick of oil

An exchange of coin

Sent into the world missing parts of myself

But strangely, more valued for its surrender

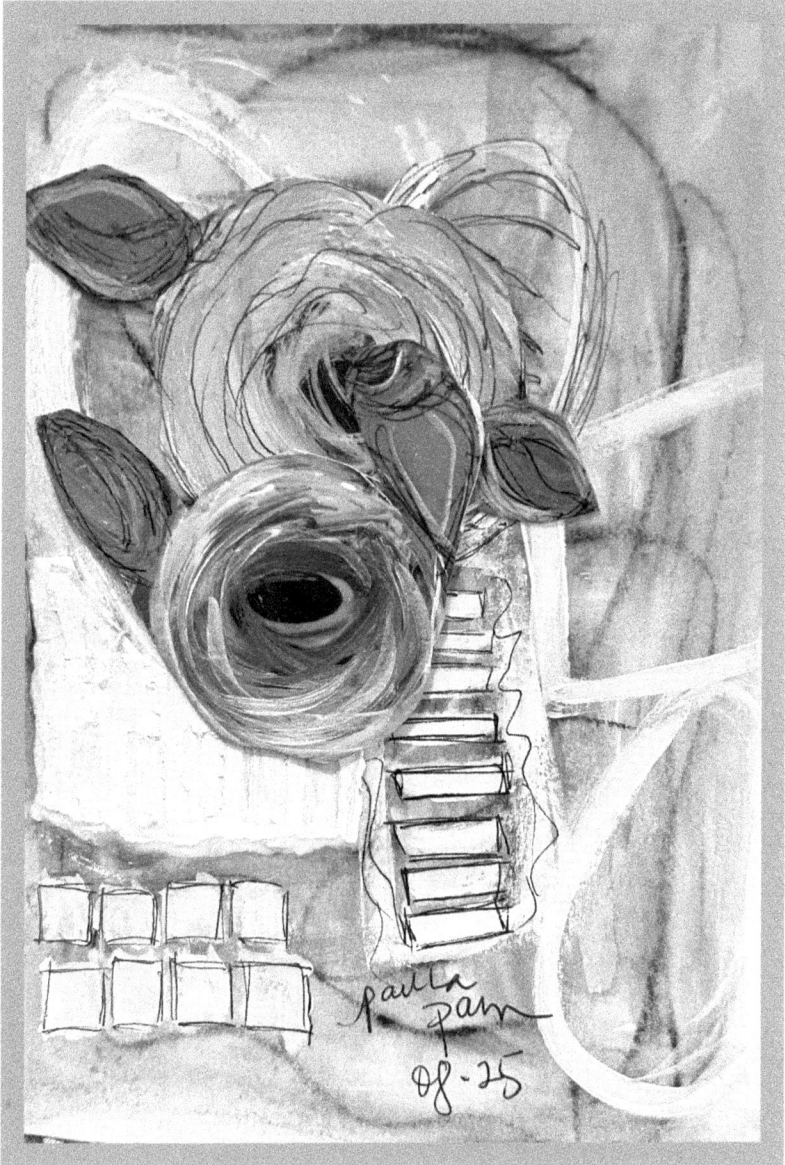

Stairway to Rose Heaven- Paula Pam Wainwright

Women's Rights, Rites, Writes

© 2025 Bonnie Bostrom,
Carla Christenson,
Michele Cuomo,
Barbara Martin,
Barbara Poirer,
Juanita Remien,
Kim Roley,
Mia Self
Paula Pam Wainwright

ISBN: 979-8-9940853-0-1

Published by:
Canelo Project
www.caneloproject.com

Book/Cover design: Athena Steen

Artwork: **Pamela Pam Wainwright**